HIDDEN TREASURES

AMAZING STORIES

FROM THE

NEW TESTAMENT

BROADMAN
&HOLMAN
PUBLISHERS

NASHVILLE, TENNESSEE

For Christy
Psalm 125:1

Copyright © 2000 by Mary Manz Simon
Illustration Copyright © 2000 by Broadman & Holman Publishers
Published in 2000 by Broadman & Holman Publishers
Nashville, Tennessee

Library of Congress Cataloging-in-Publication Data

Simon, Mary Manz, 1948-
   Hidden treasures : amazing stories from the New Testament / by Mary
Manz Simon ;
   illustrations by Jeff Preston.
      p. cm.
   ISBN 0-8054-2329-X (hardcover)
   1. Bible stories, English--N.T. [1. Bible stories--N.T.] I. Preston, Jeff,
1958- ill. II.
   Title.

   BS2401 .S46 2000
   225.9'505--dc21

                                                         00-037911

1 2 3 4 5   04 03 02 01 00

TABLE OF CONTENTS

A Very Special Gift

Zacharias trembled with anticipation. He had prepared all of his life for this moment. Now an elderly man, the moment had arrived. Today, Zacharias would enter the holy place. While the people prayed in the temple, he alone would go before the altar.

"May God go with you," Elizabeth said, reaching toward her husband. She knew the importance of this moment for Zacharias. Zacharias said nothing. No words were needed; the couple's loving embrace showed more than words could ever say.

"Is this the day?" called a friend, as Elizabeth waved goodbye to her husband.

"Yes," Elizabeth nodded. "And what a great day it is."

"Thanks be to God," said her friend.

And Elizabeth repeated, "Thanks be to God."

Elizabeth and Zacharias, a priest, had faithfully worshiped God for a very long time. They looked forward to the coming of the promised Savior. The two had shared many happy years. Their only disappointment had been that in spite of repeated prayers, they had never been given a child. But now, that sadness was momentarily forgotten in this splendid moment.

Zacharias walked deliberately to the temple. He wanted to remember every single moment of this wonderful time. He could no longer run on his aching legs, but his heart was beating as if he neared the finish line of a race. Grateful for the opportunity to serve in this special way, he praised God without stopping during his whole journey.

People at prayer glanced up briefly as the priest walked into the temple. They would stay outside, until Zacharias had finished burning incense in the holy place. Then he would come out to give them a blessing.

Finally entering the holy place, Zacharias bowed before the altar. Then he burned the incense, just as he had practiced in his head so many times. With a thankful heart, he began to pray. But suddenly a figure appeared next to the altar.

Shaking in fear, the old priest demanded. "Who would dare to enter this holy place?"

Immediately, the angel calmed him, "Do not be afraid Zacharias. I am Gabriel."

The angel continued, "God has heard your prayers. Your wife Elizabeth will have a son who will give you great joy. You must name him John."

Zacharias stared at the angel.

"How can this happen?" he asked. "My wife and I are very old. What proof can you give me?"

Gabriel answered, "I was sent to tell you this good news, but you don't believe me. So you will not be able to talk until all this happens. But I promise you, everything will happen as I said." Then Gabriel was gone.

Zacharias stared at the place where the angel had stood. As if in a daze, he left the altar. As he entered the temple, people looked up, expecting to receive their blessing. But Zacharias was speechless. He could only show with his hands what had happened in the holy place.

Months passed. Finally Elizabeth held their newborn son. Everyone was excited for the happy couple. Friends and family came from long distances to see the miracle of this child born to the elderly woman and the elderly priest.

"You must stay for the celebration," Elizabeth said to everyone. "When our son is eight days old, we will name him."

Although their home was crowded with guests, Zacharias silently continued to praise God for the blessing of a healthy birth. And Elizabeth continued to invite everyone to the special ceremony. People gathered for the celebration at which the baby would receive his name.

"He will certainly be called Zacharias, like his father," agreed several of the guests. But overhearing their conversation, Zacharias knew their son would have a different name.

Finally, Elizabeth announced the child's name.

"He will be called John," she said without hesitation. But one of the relatives immediately spoke up.

"But no one in our family has ever been called John," she said.

"Find out from Zacharias what his son should be named," suggested another.

The old priest signaled for a writing tablet. Then he wrote four words: "His name is John."

Immediately, Zacharias starting speaking. And just as quickly, Zacharias praised God.

Everyone in the room was astonished at what they had seen. They wondered who this infant would grow up to be. But they were certain that God had given Elizabeth and Zacharias a very special gift.

Based on
Luke 1:5-23; 57-66

To Talk About:

1. Ask someone to tell you the story of how your name was chosen.

2. Zacharias saw an angel. Can you think of anyone else in the Bible who saw an angel?

3. Angels are God's messengers. What message would you want God to send you?

4

Saul's Great Escape

"Step back," growled the merchant. He pushed people out of the way. "Move away. You're blocking my tables."

Today's crowd was even bigger than the one yesterday. Usually, the merchant was happy to see the marketplace filled with people. But not today: these people weren't here to buy. They came to listen.

"Move on," urged another merchant.

A few people glanced toward the angry shopkeepers, but most didn't even notice them.

People in the crowd didn't come to smell the sweet spices. They didn't want to touch the soft silks. They only wanted to hear a man preach.

"Jesus is the Lord," Saul boomed. He stood on an empty table so everyone in the courtyard could hear. "He is the Savior."

The merchants complained among themselves.

"Jesus, Jesus, Jesus," said one. "That's all these people can think about."

"No one will buy my fresh spices today," complained another.

"I haven't had a single customer look at my beautiful silks," added a grumpy merchant.

Two men stood at the edge of the crowd. They didn't have anything to sell. But they weren't happy either. They didn't want to hear about Jesus. They wanted to stop Saul from preaching.

"No sales today?" one of these men asked the merchants.

"How can we sell anything?" the merchant asked. "Everyone wants

to hear Saul talk about Jesus. They don't want to buy my ivory."

"And no one will even look at these sparkling jewels," complained another.

"Would you like to get rid of Saul?" one of the men asked.

"Oh yes," nodded the merchants eagerly.

"But how can we do that?" one quickly asked.

"Meet us here when people have gone home," suggested one of the men. "Then we'll make a plan."

After dark, when the sweet smell of the spices hung heavy in the night air, the men met at the empty marketplace. They talked quietly among themselves until their meeting ended with a happy shout. They had the perfect plan. The men would take

turns watching the city gates. Day and night, the men would guard the gates. If Saul tried to leave, he would be caught. He could not escape.

Saul preached in the market again the next day and the next. "Jesus is the Lord," he said in a loud voice. Each day the crowds grew larger. More and more people heard about Jesus.

Finally, Saul decided his work in the city was done. But how could he leave? He had heard about the plan to capture him. Saul knew he couldn't escape unless he and his friends came up with a plan of their own.

Saul and his friends worked carefully. They found long, strong ropes. They found a big basket made with thick branches. Then they waited and watched for a night when they couldn't see the moon.

Finally, on a very dark night, Saul and his friends met at the city wall. They tied the ropes onto the handles of the basket. Saul climbed in. Carefully and quietly, his friends lowered the basket over the wall.

Thump.

The basket banged against the wall.

"Be careful," Saul whispered up in the darkness. He could barely see the shadows of his friends' faces. Slowly now, ever so slowly, they lowered the basket.

Thud.

The basket hit the ground.

Squeak.

A mouse ran out from under the basket.

Saul laughed softly. Then he looked out into the dark night. Only his friends and the little mouse knew of his escape. Saul waved in the darkness toward his friends. Then he hurried away from the city wall.

Saul ran into the darkness. He escaped! He was free! He was free to preach about Jesus!

To Talk About:

1. How did God help Saul?

2. Saul trusted his friends to help him. Trust means you can count on someone. Whom do you trust?

3. Why do you think Saul kept preaching about Jesus, even when he knew it might be dangerous?

A Knock at the Door

"Please come for conversation after dinner," Mary said politely to the shopkeeper weighing the lentils.

"Yes, I'll see you tonight," he said, handing Mary her purchase. Pleased that her secret message had been delivered, Mary quickly faded into the crowd at the busy marketplace. She, her son John Mark, and the other Christians needed to be very careful. This was such a dangerous time. King Herod had already killed James, one of Jesus' helpers. Now another helper, Peter, was in prison. Tomorrow, Peter was scheduled to be tried in court. Mary must contact Jesus' followers immediately so they could pray without stopping all through the night.

Pausing by another stall in the market, Mary inspected some cucumbers. Then her mind drifted back to the meeting scheduled for her home. Mary knew she could be arrested for hosting the group of Christians tonight. King Herod could even demand that she be killed.

"May I help you?" asked the shopkeeper, interrupting her thoughts.

"Nothing today," said Mary. "But please come for conversation after dinner."

"Yes, I'll see you tonight," he responded to Mary's coded message. The merchant had prayed all day. He knew Peter was in grave danger. With a heavy heart, he moved to serve his next customer.

After dark, the guests began to drift into Mary's home for what she had called "conversation." But those who were invited knew they would not be talking among themselves; instead, they would have long conversations with God. Bending to kneel, the guests began to pray that God would protect Peter. His situation was desperate: every person in the room knew only God could help Peter.

Knock, knock came a rapping at the courtyard gate.

Puzzled, Mary looked up. Everyone was here. Had King Herod's soldiers found out about their prayer meeting? She ignored the knocking, and continued to pray.

Knock, knock. The rapping persisted.

Motioning young Rhoda toward the gate, Mary bowed her head once again.

Rhoda walked to the courtyard gate. Rhoda was puzzled, too. Who would be knocking at this time of night? All their friends had arrived hours earlier. Peering through the latch in the door, a familiar face stared back through the darkness. Stunned and speechless, Rhoda re-latched the gate and hurried across the courtyard.

Swallowing hard, because she knew how strange her message would sound, Rhoda tugged on Mary's gown.

"It's Peter," Rhoda whispered. "Peter's at the gate."

Shaking her head at Rhoda's interruption, Mary continued to pray.

"It's Peter," Rhoda repeated a little louder. "Peter's at the gate."

Glancing up with frustration, Mary said, "Peter is in prison. Come back and join us in prayer."

"No, no," Rhoda insisted in an even louder tone of voice. "Peter is at the gate."

"Shhh," quieted one of the praying guests. "We could be killed for being here."

Others had overheard the young girl, and looked up from their conversations with God.

"You're crazy Rhoda," one of them said.

Another said somewhat fearfully, "If that's Peter's ghost, perhaps King Herod has already killed him."

Knock, knock.

"A ghost wouldn't knock," said Rhoda.

Getting up from her knees, Mary said, "I'll go with you." Together, the women walked to the courtyard gate.

Opening the latch slightly, Mary and Rhoda stared at the face peering through the darkness.

"Peter?" Mary squeaked, unable to believe who she was seeing.

Mary yanked open the gate. Peter stepped inside from the dark street, and quickly latched the gate shut behind him.

Motioning the women to be silent, Peter walked across the courtyard to the prayer group.

In whispered tones, Peter told of how God had freed him from prison. Amazed, his friends could only marvel at the great God they served. Everyone gave thanks for Peter's freedom. Then one by one, they slipped out of Mary's home and returned to their own houses. While it was still dark, Peter escaped to another safe place.

Based on
Acts 12:1-17

To Talk About:

1. Why were the Christians afraid?

2. What good decision did Mary and her friends make?

3. Peter surprised his friends. Perhaps God surprised Peter by freeing him from jail! Has God ever surprised you?

Jesus and the Children

People hurried past. They were eager to get up the hillside. Jesus' helpers moved back and watched.

"There are even more people coming today," said one of Jesus' helpers, astonished at the crowd gathering in front of them.

"That's amazing," said another. "I thought yesterday would be the biggest crowd we'd ever see."

"It's wonderful so many people want to learn from the Master, but I'm afraid Jesus is getting tired," said one of His helpers. "He teaches from morning to night."

"And the people seem to be crowding up closer each time He preaches," another observed.

"Our Master needs space to breathe," said another. "Let's keep the people farther back from Him today."

Jesus' helpers moved forward to follow their plan, but the hillside was already packed with people. Some sat on boulders. Others crowded into spaces between bushes. The crush of people moved ever closer to Jesus, eager to hear what He was saying.

A group of parents moved along the outer edge of the crowd. They had hoped Jesus could bless their babies and young children. But there wasn't even room to step among the people.

"Jesus?" asked one little boy, looking up at his mother.

"Let me pick you up," she answered. "Then you can see Him better."

"Jesus?" said the boy.

"Yes," his mother nodded. "I want Jesus to give you a blessing." Settling her son into her arms, the little boy promptly fell asleep. He woke up just as Jesus finished speaking.

Even though Jesus had ended His teaching for the day, the crowd did not move down the hillside. Instead, people edged closer and closer to the boulder where Jesus now sat to rest. Reaching out, He blessed everyone who came within reach.

"Let's go up there, too," urged a mother holding the hand of two little girls. "We've been here all day and the children will get fussy if we wait much longer."

As if a baby understood what the woman said, a wail went up from one of the infants. Soon, other tired and hungry children added their voices to an increasingly noisy scene. But slowly the parents made their way up the hill. The parents and children gradually filled in the empty spaces left by those who had received a blessing. Finally the parents caught close-up glimpses of Jesus. And everyone heard the group of children getting closer to the

top.

"The Master is tired," said one of His helpers, stopping a mother as she moved up the hillside. "He can't bother with children."

Quickly another of Jesus' helpers came to tell the parents to turn around and go down the hill.

"We've waited all day," protested one of the parents. "We want Jesus to give our children a blessing."

"He doesn't have time for children," one of the helpers repeated sternly.

"We want our children to see Jesus," said a mother, who held firmly to the hand of a fussy toddler.

This commotion, which was taking place so near Jesus, was beginning to attract attention. Soon, even the Master looked over to see what was happening.

Sliding off the boulder, Jesus stretched out His arms toward the group of waiting parents and children. Older people moved away, as Jesus motioned again to the children. Clearing off a space on the ground, He encouraged the parents to bring the younger ones to Him. Jesus told His helpers, "Let them come here."

"There is one more lesson today," he explained. "And these children will help me teach."

Puzzled, Jesus' helpers stepped back. "How can a child help the Master teach?" one man wondered aloud.

Jesus then looked into the eager little faces that peered up at Him. He hugged the small ones who stood close by. Smiling at them all, Jesus asked, "Do you see the trust in these young faces?"

Looking around at the children, even His helpers nodded.

"People who have the kind of hope and love of young children are the people who belong to God," said Jesus.

Still seated on the ground, Jesus reached out to each child. Then He stood and blessed every infant. Grateful parents thanked Him.

As Jesus walked among the families, He repeated, "The Kingdom of God is made of people who are like these children."

Based on Luke 18:15-17

To Talk About:

1. How did Jesus show His helpers that children are important people?

2. What activities and programs does your church offer just for children?

3. The children probably felt very special when Jesus took time to bless them. Talk about a time when you felt special.

A War of Words

W hew," said the servant girl, wrinkling her nose. "Today's catch stinks."

"At least the fish are fresh," said the other servant, shifting her basket of grapes.

"This is the favorite part of my work," said her companion. "Except like today when the fish smell as if they jumped out of the net into my basket!"

"I agree," nodded the other servant. "It's nice to give such good food to those poor women."

Each day, servants from the homes of wealthier families would take food to the widows of the church. Some days the women would receive honey, dates, or olives. Other days, the widows would get sacks of barley so they could make bread. The food was delivered to one location, then shared among the needy.

Today though, as the servants neared the meeting place, they could hear angry voices. It sounded like people were yelling at each other in different languages.

As the servants turned the corner, they could see that was exactly what was happening. Older women under the tent were arguing with other women outside the tent. The women in both groups were gesturing wildly, as it was obvious from the war of words that they didn't speak the same language. Several church leaders moved among the women, attempting to calm them. Standing to the side, the servants waited quietly to see what would happen. Gradually, the yelling stopped and the groups of widows glared at each

other. Some church leaders talked with the women under the tent; other leaders talked
with the widows on the street. Finally, the men met together.

Two of the leaders stepped forward.

"God has instructed us to care for the widows among us," he said. The other man translated the words into a second language.

Gesturing toward the servant girls, one of the men said, "We are grateful that each day,
food is brought to our widows in need."

As the second man translated these words, a calm gradually fell over both groups of
women.

"Every person here believes that Jesus Christ is Lord," he said. "Right now, we should be
out in the streets sharing that message. We shouldn't waste time arguing among our-

selves about who gets the figs and who gets the raisins."

As the women recognized the truth in these words, some appeared embarrassed. Others merely looked away or down at the ground, as if to apologize for their selfishness.

"But it's obvious we need to develop a better way to provide for the widows in our church," he summed up. "Before we leave to tell others about Jesus this morning, we will help divide the food. Tomorrow when you return here, we will have a better plan."

Quietly, the women filed past the men, carrying their empty baskets and pots. The widows, who had just been reminded of their blessings, received the food with thanks. When all the food had been distributed, the men gathered to discuss the problem.

The next morning, the servant girls once again headed for the widows' meeting site.

"Today you have the stinky basket," smiled one of the servants.

Her friend laughed. "At least oysters don't flop their tails in my face, but the widows really liked your fish yesterday."

"Yes," nodded her companion. "Seriously though, this morning I prayed that God would heal the trouble between those women."

"I wonder what solution the church leaders came up with?" said the servant girl.

"We'll soon see," said her friend as they neared the tent. Widows and church leaders were waiting. Only a quiet murmur was heard as the widows looked eagerly to see what the servants had brought today. Everyone waited patiently to hear what the church leaders had decided.

"We have two kinds of work to do," began one man. He waited while another translated his words.

"We must preach God's message, and care for those in need. We must care for people like the widows here this morning." Nodding to the translator, he waited for him to speak the same words.

"Seven godly men have been chosen to see that your everyday needs are met," he explained. "That will leave us free to continue praying, preaching, and teaching about Jesus Christ."

As the women thought about the plan, many nodded. Some began talking among themselves. The widows joined in thanking God for their blessings. And as the leaders spread the good news about Jesus, more people joined the church.

Based on Acts 6:1-6

To Talk About:

1. Have you ever helped someone who was needy? Talk about it.

2. How did you feel to hear a story about Christians arguing with other Christians?

3. Talk about a disagreement you've had with someone.

A Lucky Guy?

Eutychus was stuck. He was jammed in tight. So many people wanted to hear Paul talk about Jesus, the whole crowd was unable to move. And Eutychus was caught in the middle. He couldn't move up the stairs. He couldn't move down the stairs. And because he was shorter than the grown-ups, he couldn't even see.

Then he looked down.

"I can crawl," he thought. "I'm still young." So carefully, Eutychus slid to the ground and crawled up the stairs. He scrambled past hairy legs and legs covered in beautiful cloth. Up and up he went, one stair at a time. Finally, he reached the top.

"Now what?" Eutychus wondered. He tried to look across the room, but torches filled the air with oily smoke. Eutychus could hardly see beyond a few people sitting on the floor. "Stay low in smoke," he remembered a teacher saying. So Eutychus started to crawl around the room.

"Excuse me," murmured Eutychus, as he crawled around a big man with a beard.

"Excuse me," whispered Eutychus, as he crawled over long legs.

"Ouch."

Eutychus rubbed his head. He had crawled right into the wall. He felt a bump rise on his forehead, then looked at the troublesome wall. He had banged into a wall with a window. What a perfect place to sit! He pulled

himself up to the small opening. "Just the right fit for a little guy like me," he thought.

Eutychus waved the smoky haze away from his face. Now he could see Paul in the center of the room. Others stood nearby with food.

"This is my lucky night," he thought. "I found a seat, I get to hear Paul, and I'll get some food."

Soon, Paul started talking. Eutychus listened as Paul talked about Jesus, the Savior. Eutychus listened as Paul talked about praying to God.

Eutychus started to nod "Yes" each time Paul said something about Jesus. Eutychus started nodding a lot. He yawned. Eutychus closed his eyes. He nodded again.

Crash.

"Someone fell," yelled a man, looking through the small hole in the wall.

"Somebody fell out the window."

Eutychus lay flat on the ground.

He was still.

He wasn't moving.

People pushed through the crowd. The first man to reach Eutychus said, "He's dead. He's dead."

Another man listened for a heartbeat. He couldn't hear anything.

Another watched for Eutychus to breathe. His chest didn't seem to move.

Then the men stepped back.

Paul had come. He knelt down. Paul lifted Eutychus into his arms and said, "He is alive."

Eutychus' eyes fluttered open. He was helped up. Leaning on others, Eutychus went back up the stairs. He ate supper. And he whispered his own prayer.

"Tonight I was not lucky. I was blessed. God blessed me."

Based on Acts 20:7-12

To Talk About:

1. What happened to Eutychus?

2. Eutychus learned about Jesus from St. Paul. Who tells you about Jesus?

3. How did God bless Eutychus?

Riot in the City

"Blessed," said Paul to no one in particular. "That's how I feel today. Blessed by God."

Today was the third Sabbath in a row that Paul would preach about Jesus in the city of Thessalonica. He was grateful that so many people were learning about Jesus. He was grateful to be in a waterside city once again, where he could smell the fresh air as it blew across the gulf. And Paul appreciated the hospitality of Jason, who had welcomed him into his home.

When Paul reached the meeting area, people were already there to greet him. Although it was early, Paul could see that more listeners than ever would come to hear him. After preaching about Jesus, Paul returned to Jason's home, very glad to have such a quiet place to rest.

But across town, things were not as calm and peaceful. Some of the religious leaders, upset with Paul's message that "Jesus is Lord," were stirring up trouble.

Clink, clink, clink, clink, clink. A shower of coins funneled rapidly into the open money bag.

"That's your pay for starting the riot," explained one of the religious leaders. "Make sure you cause enough trouble to get a big mob."

The rough-looking men nodded.

"Don't worry," assured one of the hired hands. "We'll cause plenty of problems."

"Starting a riot sure beats hanging out at the marketplace all day," joked

his partner.

Yells and shouts were soon heard along the waterfront. Fights started in the streets. Brawls began on the wharfs. And as anticipated, a large unruly mob gathered in the city center. The hired hands had done their job.

Hearing the commotion, Jason began to worry. Perhaps the popularity of Paul's teaching had triggered some of the unrest. If that was true, Paul faced immediate danger. Concerned about Paul's safety, Jason quickly gathered a group of Christians to escort the preacher to a temporary hiding place.

"Stay hidden until night," Jason advised him. "Then under cover of darkness, head toward Berea."

Quickly Paul and the small group hurried down back streets. Jason breathed a sigh of

relief as they disappeared from sight. Paul had escaped - and not a moment too soon.

The religious leaders were already headed toward Jason's home. They were so jealous of Paul and the big crowds he was attracting that they wanted to be sure he and his helpers were thrown to the mob and roughed up. They pounded heavily at the door until Jason came to greet them.

Rushing past Jason, they strode through every room.

"Where is he?" one of the ringleaders asked. "Where are you hiding Paul?"

"Paul isn't here now," said Jason truthfully. He and the other Christians had helped Paul escape just before the religious leaders arrived.

Yet the men tore through the house. They overturned every piece of furniture. They ripped apart every bed, looking for Paul. Not willing to leave empty-handed, they collared Jason and yanked him off with the other Christians. Jason and the others were dragged through the streets and finally tossed to the ground in front of city leaders.

"Look who we got here," growled one of the religious leaders. "Jason, who's hosting that troublemaker Paul."

"He's one of the guys who says Jesus is Lord," accused another.

The city officials looked at each other. This was upsetting news. Jason was called to stand before the authorities. Then he was asked a single question.

"Do you believe Jesus is Lord?" the men asked.

"Yes, I believe," said Jason without hesitation.

One by one, each of the other Christians was asked the same question. One by one, each responded firmly, "Yes, I believe."

The city officials could not let people break the laws of the emperor, so Jason and the others were charged a fee. After paying bail, they were freed that night and allowed to return to their homes. Across town, under the cover of darkness, Paul escaped for the second time that day.

Based on
Acts 17:1-15

To Talk About:

1. Why were the religious leaders jealous of Paul?

2. How did God take care of Paul?

3. How does God take care of you?

A Change of Heart

Matthew smiled as he hurried down the road. He was eager to begin another day of work. His office was near the lake, and Matthew was getting close enough to smell the moist air. "Ahh," he sighed, breathing deeply. Matthew liked working near the waterfront. He liked the noise and excitement of boats going in and out. Something was always happening. Today even more people than usual were gathered on the sandy beach. Matthew moved quickly through the crowd, because there was something he liked more than the sea. Matthew was a tax collector. He loved money.

"Clink, clink, clink," thought Matthew. His heart pounded, just thinking about the coins he would collect today. "I really love money." He smiled to himself.

It wasn't long before the money started piling up on his table. Matthew scooped coins into bags tucked under his chair. Soon, the heavy bags of

money completely surrounded his feet. A money bag even became his footstool.

As more people came to pay taxes, a line formed around his table. People began to grumble. The line grew longer. Children started to fuss.

Suddenly, the grumbling stopped.

The children were quiet.

There wasn't a sound.

Matthew looked up from his table. What was happening? Was a robber hiding in the crowd? Was there a thief? Was someone coming to steal his money?

Quickly, Matthew grabbed a handful of coins. Nobody was going to get the money.

Matthew picked up more coins, then glanced up for just a moment. A man stood before him. Matthew looked into the face of Jesus.

The children were silent.

The crowd was hushed.

Then Jesus said two words to Matthew: "Follow Me."

Matthew felt his palms begin to sweat. The heavy coins were making his arms ache in a most wonderful way. He could imagine the clink of that glorious money when he took it home to count. But then, in a quiet whisper, Matthew repeated the words Jesus had said, "Follow Me."

Clunk.

The coins fell to the ground as Matthew stood up.

"There is more to life than money," Matthew suddenly realized. Jesus loved him. As Jesus started to walk away, a small child touched his robe and said softly, "Hello, Jesus." Jesus bent down to ruffle the boy's hair and turned His head ever so slightly to look back. Matthew was following right behind.

Based on Mark 2: 13-14

To Talk About:

1. Matthew loved money more than anything. Whom does God say we should love more than anything?

2. Do you think it was hard or easy for Matthew to leave his money and follow Jesus? Why?

3. Matthew became one of Jesus' helpers. How do people know you are Jesus' helper?

Joy in Jail

Silas peered through the darkness. He could hardly see where he was going. Stumbling, he tried to feel with his feet for the next step, but the prison guard shoved him down many steps at once. Banging into the cold wet walls, the damp darkness surrounded him. Soon Silas found himself chained in the stinking basement of the city jail.

"Paul," he whispered, hoping his missionary friend was nearby.

"Paul?"

"I'm over here," Paul said.

"Praise God I'm not alone," Silas said. "I can't see you in the darkness."

"But I am here and God is here," Paul said. "You aren't alone, my friend."

In spite of his chains and bruises, Silas was relieved to hear his friend's voice. Silas also appreciated Paul's reminder. He and Paul had been traveling together, telling people about Jesus. God had blessed their work. Every day, more people learned that Jesus was Lord. Silas was confident that God would continue to take care of them, even in prison."

"Let's pray," suggested Paul. "Let's ask God to be with the slave girl we helped today."

"Yes and to be with us in this horrible place," Silas added. He couldn't see what was crawling around his legs, but he didn't like the creepy feeling.

Quietly, the men began to pray. Then Paul began to sing.

"Hey you," interrupted a shaky voice from the darkness.

Stopping, Paul and Silas listened.

"What are you singing about?" the voice asked.

"We're thanking God for being with us here," answered Silas. "It's good to know that even in prison, we're not alone."

As Paul again started praising God, Silas thought of the incredible God they served. Even in this smelly place with creepy, crawly things all around, people could still learn about the one true God. Even in jail, he could be joyful.

Hours passed; Paul and Silas still sang to God. Then Silas felt as if the floor started to roll underneath him. The wall shook behind him. The chains rattled at his feet. As the earthquake rumbled through the prison, Silas was thrown to the ground. A heavy cell door

crashed down so close to him he could feel the splinters sail through the thick air. His chains had come loose.

"Paul, I'm free, I'm free," Silas spoke into the darkness. "Where are you?"

"Here I am," called his friend.

A light flickered in the darkness, as the jailer made his way down the crumbled stairway. Holding his lantern high, he was amazed at the sight. Cell doors were flung open or were hanging limply on broken hinges. Bars had crashed apart and lay scattered on the ground. Loose chains littered the cracked floor. Stunned, the jailer realized what had happened: All the prisoners had been freed during the earthquake.

Terrified, the jailer pulled out his sword.

"Don't hurt yourself or anyone else," said Paul. "No one has escaped. We're all still here."

In the dim light, the jailer looked at Paul and Silas. He knew then that they were not evil men. Falling at their feet, the jailer begged, "How can I be saved?"

"Believe in the Lord Jesus Christ and you will be saved," they answered. The jailer's heart filled with joy. Standing uneasily on the broken floor, he reached out toward the missionaries.

"Come, you must come home with me," he invited. "Please tell my family about Jesus."

Following his dim light up the cracked stairway, Paul and Silas picked their way past the rubble. When they entered the home, even though it was the middle of the night, the missionaries told the jailer's family about Jesus. Lanterns were lit, and family members cared for Paul and Silas. They ate wonderful food. The house was filled with bright light and discussions about Jesus. Before the night ended, everyone in the household believed that Jesus was the one true God.

Based on Acts 16:16-40

To Talk About:

1. Paul and Silas were persecuted because they taught about Jesus. "Persecuted" means that you get in trouble for what you believe. After hearing this story, how do you feel about how the missionaries were persecuted?

2. Why could Paul and Silas be joyful in jail?

3. How did God help His missionaries?

Shipwrecked!

Waves rippled in the gentle breeze. The autumn air hinted at the approaching season, but today the sea was calm.

"Winter storms are coming," Paul warned the captain again. But the man was eager to deliver grain to the final port. At the ship's meeting last night, Paul had spoken against sailing so late into the season, but he could see his words had no effect. Already, the sailors were scrambling around the masts, preparing to sail.

Paul planted his feet firmly on the rolling deck. This was the third ship on which he had sailed recently, and he now felt as comfortable on the sea as any sailor. Paul was traveling to Rome as a prisoner under armed guard. There he would be tried in court.

Watching the coast disappear from view, Paul still stood on deck. Although he was concerned about the safety of this voyage, he was confident God would be with him.

Once at sea, whitecaps appeared on the water. Gusts of wind whipped the upper deck. The first of the winter storms had hit.

"You should have listened to me," Paul called to the captain. Attempting to steer away from the storm which now raged around them, the captain didn't even hear Paul. He was struggling to rescue the lifeboat.

"Grab hold," called the captain. "Grab hold now."

"I can't get it," yelled a sailor. "We've got to try again."

Finally the crew dragged the lifeboat onto the deck. Then, fighting the stinging rain and vicious wind, they tied heavy cables to hold the boat together in the swelling sea. To lighten the load, they threw extra weights and tackle overboard. Paul watched as extra crates and bundles were tossed out and quickly disappeared beneath the high waves. Even though Paul was traveling as a prisoner, the guards barely paid attention to him. No one could escape in this storm.

Day was almost as dark as night. The captain could not see a single star or catch a glimpse of sun or moon to help him steer. Day followed endless day. Night after night the storm continued.

Bracing himself on the wildly rolling deck, Paul made his way to the captain.

"You and the crew must take time to eat," Paul encouraged. "We've all been without food for so long, we will only get weaker."

Nodding to a crew member, the captain reluctantly left the wheel. He knew Paul had been right to warn him about traveling at this time of year. But now, there was nothing to do but hold on tight.

"Captain, you and your crew will be safe," Paul encouraged. "God will be with all of us, every one of the 276 people on this ship."

Even though Paul was a prisoner, the captain had a growing respect for the missionary. Encouraged by Paul's words and strengthened by the food, the captain returned to the top deck.

"Land ahoy," went the shout.

Peering into the brightening sky, everyone on board crowded to the side of the ship. A slip of land appeared on the horizon. The crew threw the anchors overboard to again lighten the ship. High above the main deck, the sail was unfurled and the ship headed toward shore. But as they entered shallow waters, one end of the ship got stuck in the sand. Waves beat against the other end of the boat. A huge wave washed over the ship, breaking off pieces of the deck. Still another wave drenched the decks. Piece by piece, the ship was being ripped apart by the powerful sea.

"Kill the prisoners," yelled the soldiers who were guarding Paul and the others. "We can't allow the prisoners to escape."

"No," commanded the captain. "Everyone, swim for your lives."

As the ship broke apart, guards, prisoners, and crew were tossed into the angry waters. Some sailors grabbed onto pieces of lumber. Others rode on top of crates. Others simply tried to stay afloat as waves crashed around them. A cold rain fell from they sky and the furious sea churned beneath them.

One by one, people dragged onto the beach. Soon, all the travelers had reached land. Paul had been right: every one of the 276 people aboard would be saved. Once again, God had cared for His people. Paul spent the next weeks praying, thanking, and serving God, who had been with them on the terrible journey, saved them from the shipwreck, and brought them safely to land.

Based on Acts 27

To Talk About:

1. Do you think Paul was afraid during the terrible storm? Talk about it.

2. Paul was a missionary. A missionary tells people about God. Have you ever told someone about God?

3. What was the best part of this story?